QUILTING MADE EASY

PERFECT QUILTING FOR BEGINNERS

JAMIE J.

CONTENTS

Introduction	1
Quilting	2
Different Quilting	5
Accessorized Quilting	8
Ways of Template Making	10
Tips on Making Templates	12
Designing a Quilt	14
Quilting in Negative Blank Space	16
Complex Quilt Blocks	19
Sneak Peek - Chapter 1	22

©Copyright 2022 – All rights reserved by Jamie J.

The content of this book may not be reproduced, duplicated, or transmitted without direct written permission from the author or publisher.

ISBN: 978-1-63970-137-7

Legal Notice:

This book is copyright protected. This is only for personal use. You cannot amend, distribute, sell, use, quote, or paraphrase any part of the content within this book without the consent of the author or publisher.

Disclaimer notice:

Please note the information contained within this document is for educational and entertainment purposes only.

Every attempt has been made to provide accurate, up-to-date, and reliable complete information.

No warranties of any kind are expressed or implied. Readers acknowledge that the author is not engaging in the rendering of legal, financial, medical or professional advice. The content of this book has been derived from various sources. Please consult a licensed professional before attempting any techniques outlined in this book.

By reading this document, the reader agrees that under no circumstances is the author responsible for any losses, direct or indirect, which are incurred as a result of the use of the information contained within this document, including, but not limited to, -errors, omissions, or inaccuracies.

❦ Created with Vellum

INTRODUCTION

Welcome aboard this quilting training for Kindle. Quilting is an art where two layers of fiber will be brought together. It is an art that has been practiced for ages, and I believe it will become easy for anyone who has been giving it a wide berth. The many decorations that we see are a product of this art. And since machines are being used, one needs to give it a stab and see how it evolves. But since the process cannot be done without using hands, thread, or needles through the coordinated brain mechanisms, I believe it will be easy. A quilter will make little and reproducible stitches in this art just like a laborious ant and come out an expert. I hope you will enjoy reading it.

QUILTING

Talking Point 1: Definition of Quilting

Concisely described, a quilted product of two layers of cloth, each filled up with bandage-like material and later stitched together. It is also an art of stitching in which these materials known as quilts come handy in the manufacture of decorative designs. Mainly a hand exercise, quilting has become an art where machines are also used. Quilting is carried out on a chassis called a frame in quilting terms, and this chassis is called a quilting hoop. But the process cannot be complete without thread or needles designed purposely for quilting. A quilter must be adept at using both hands since one hand will be fully engaged in the stitching process while the other takes care of the quilting needle. In this art, a quilter will make tiny and reproducible stitches. However, it is worth noting that the stitches should be straight and consistent in whatever form they are.

Quilt Lining (Backing)

. . .

When one turns over a quilt, a backside of the lining portion of the quilted garment appears. This is what is tagged in quilting as backing. These two terms, backing or lining, are used interchangeably in the knitting world.

Talking Point 2: Different Ways of Machine Quilting Walking Foot

Quilting, the ordinary textile machine, is readily employed. This textile machine has an appliance that is tagged walking foot. It facilitates the smooth in-feeding of quilting cloth through the device. It is a piece of technology that a beginner should learn how to use effectively.

Talking Point 3: Freehanded Motion

Freehanded motion is a style that goes hand-in-hand with the application of the textile machine in quilting. This style is evidenced when a darn foot is employed. One great advantage with this style is in the corresponding textile used when quilting takes place. A quilter using a machine will match yarn and the garment to produce a quality finished product. Since the corresponding of the above two becomes a tough act, a thin thread is a preferably made use of, known as monofilament. Two styles deliver a variety of quality-designed products. Like in all manufacturing, where names are used as identification, these products are shadow-lined. A beginner should note that a textile machine produces different shadow-lined products compared to those hand-quilted.

If a quilting enthusiast takes a critical look at these different products, he will note that the ones done by hand have modest lines. They also have speckles with wrinkled lines. But the machine-made ones will show crooked lines. On the other side, a look at one done by a machine reveals straightened lines.

Still, on comparative grounds, hand-knitted ones are touchy and soft with different faces, and so people prefer these hand-knitted ones to the textile-machine manufactured ones. But from a tasty kind of approach, these two styles have their enthusiasts, with each group basing their support on the quality of the end products.

DIFFERENT QUILTING

Talking Point 1: Ditching

As commonly referred to by quilters, ditching is done on the undersurface of a seam formation or line. It is a style in quilting. By now, a quilter should have known that a seam formation does not have seam adjustments or allowance. One cannot tell if there are any adjustments since it is invisible except at a very closer look. To a layman, ditching means sewing at the confluence or meeting of two quilt garments. It involves pressing two-seam adjustments on one end while stitches are fabricated on the other side of the seam using a layer of the garment. But the process further involves opening up the stitches that were fabricated in the center.

This technique is cheaper and very effective to a beginner simply because it follows the line or course of patching. The Video Link below demonstrates ditching:

www.youtube.com/watch?v=-LgYBUpRYeU

Talking Point 2: Echoing or Linear Quilting

. . .

Echoing is also another of the different types of knitting, which is also called linear quilting or outline. A quilter will abruptly end with the original or earlier line of a stitch in this stitching, hence the outline of linear stitching. But the quilter may advance the stitching by introducing an extra line far off the first one though in uniformity, therefore creating an echo in reference to the linear one.

This is a style that bypasses seam formation or allowance but enhances the quality of the quilted garment. Linear quilting is fast as a style since no markings are necessary, but it boosts quilting patterns on one end appliqué on the other. Based on these qualities, it has become a better option for micro-speckling-type-of-stitching. Every machine quilter must master this method whose styles outdo the others as a freehanded Moreover, as a basic style of quilting, practical application by hand or machine is acceptable.

The video link shows echo quilting:

www.youtube.com/watch?v=nxLnnvPLbWg

Motif-Themed Quilting

Motif-themed-quilting is a style that comes after patterned lines of a design perched at the quilt's apex. This pattern is usually appropriate in the making of the designs could be plumes and bowknots. Motif-themed-quilting is also labeled as block-square-embroidery or quilting. Its distinctive feature is like an ox-bow lake in a big river. Technically, it is a small engagement in a robust body of work. Motifs-themed quilts come as small bits of work at a given time and later conjoined together in doing greater works such as blanket-making and in square production like the granny squared pieces. In motif-themed quilting, the quilter has the freedom to revolve, spread out and create the difference in quality figures and other attractive compositions. The quilter again determines the size of these products, but a beginner should be informed of the same size of all motifs at the beginning of a project. But what counts at the end of the project is the stitch-pattern variance in every motif-themed quilted piece. Apart from the same size of the motifs, other qualities will play a central role, including the engraining of the piece, stitch-approach pattern, and the aesthetic appeal of each garment based on its color. Motif-themed products like political-party-slogan materials have their role in society since vital messages are passed over to convict and convince the masses to act in the path illustrated by these products. This video link shows motif-themed quilting:

www.youtube.com/watch?v=AGxiYgpDwZs

ACCESSORIZED QUILTING

Talking Point 1: Quilting in Accent

Quilting in accent comes in a hyped-up role as an accompaniment. Quilting in accent has no originality but comes in strongly in support of echoing or motif-themed styles of quilting. Only that it is not bound to pursue the already established seam formations or lines but rather comes as a color-addition style to the already established quilt. This video link shows accent quilting: www.mccallsquilting.com/blogs/.../accent-on-amish-quilt-along-begins/

Talking Point 2: Exclusive and Fill-up Quilting

Exclusive quilting, also termed 'selective,' comes in as partial quilting because only specific portions of patterns are engaged to stress or punctuate a garment. In fill-up knitting, its unique role is to bring out the beauty in garments whose base is flat.

. . .

Taking Point 3: Channelized and Crosshatched Quilting

As the name goes, channelized quilting is carried out in straight-away, parallel-of-latitude lines, but these parallel-of-latitude or straight lines are quilted in a grid-like design in crosshatched style. The position that the grid must-have can be parallel or perpendicular. So the shape of the quilted fabric will be squarely matched in nature or will take the shape of cut diamonds at the intersection of the lines in the garment. Cloths that carry these crisscross designs are a product of the creatively intertwined spatial arrangement of lines.

In meander-quilting, the process is done haphazardly and in arched shaping on the quilted garment. The quilter will also use spins and eddies to come up with the desired shapes. In its haphazard manipulations, only the quilter's mastery will create the desired quality since none of the quilted lines are supposed to crisis-cross or contact each other.

Stipple-quilting has all the similarities with echoing. It also carries traits of meander-quilting, where a garment is fully flattened in either of the respective stitches.

All-around quilting is also termed as "allover" in quilting circles. In this all-around style, a pattern in a garment has its entire pinnacle or top fully quilted but is similar in crosshatched quilting where seam lines are disregarded.

Therefore, it is worth noting by the beginner that the application of hands or textile can effectively manage all the discussed styles.

WAYS OF TEMPLATE MAKING

Talking Point 1: Template Making

Rotary cutters reign supreme in today's world of quilting. The ruler and a cutting mat make the list of the basic quilting tools in this cutting of fabric. That notwithstanding, quilt templates are still used today. Often, they are the most useful and effective way of creating blocks with odd sizes and irregular shapes.

So what is a quilt template? This is a shaped piece of material that's used as an outline for tracing during quilting. To form quilt blocks, specific templates are traced and cut out. Many types of templates are made out of many different types of materials. A beginner can use paper but has proved to be weak and not able to endure multiple tracings. Therefore heavier and durable weight materials are much more practical. Among the hardy ones include poster board, cardboard, plastic and acrylic items.

Making templates is not rocket science, but it can be easily made. The beauty of making hardy ones is that they can be used for a long time. This should be part of the training of beginners in quilt making.

. . .

Talking Point 2: Cardboard

The beginner should gather materials which include a pattern, cardboard made from boxes of cereals or rice, a marker, and a pair of small scissors.

The beginner starts by cutting out the pattern pieces. These days, quilters prefer not to cut out the actual pattern from a magazine or book but photocopy the pattern pages before finally cutting out all of those pieces.

Step three involves tearing open the cardboard boxes. Experience has shown that the best box to use is the single-layer type that holds food rather than the large, heavy-duty boxes. Boxes with a blank interior are perfect for template-making.

Tracing the pattern shapes onto the cardboard is what follows. Labeling each piece and transferring the pattern markings to each piece ensues. Finally, the beginner cuts out templates using a small pair of sharp scissors.

Talking Point 3: Plastic

In this template making, the materials include a pattern, plastic template, marker, and pair of scissors. Plastics are found in rectangular and square sheets where they are readily found in the local quilt shop. The plastic template should be laid directly over the pattern. It is also wise to tape the sheet down if need be. Finally, the beginner should trace the pattern pieces onto the plastic with a marker, and eventually, the markings should be transferred from the pattern pieces and labeled. The final stage is to remove the pieces of paper.

TIPS ON MAKING TEMPLATES

Talking Point 1: Reading Pattern Directions

In this template making, apart from a pattern, others include a plastic template, marker, and a pair of scissors. Plastics come in rectangular or square sheets and can be purchased in the local quilt shop or craft store. The plastic template should be laid directly over the pattern. It is also wise to tape the sheet down if need be. Finally, the beginner should trace the pattern pieces onto the plastic with a marker, and eventually, the markings should be transferred from the pattern pieces and labeled. The result is cutting out the pieces with a pair of small, sharp scissors.

Talking Point 2: Seam Allowance

Another detail that the beginner should take keen in is that not all templates include seam allowances. One should read the pattern carefully to see if there's a need to add more. When it comes to permanent markers, one with a fine point works perfectly during tracing. There's no provision for guesswork, so using a ruler is paramount, particularly when tracing pieces with long, straight edges. In storage of the pattern templates, they should be labeled and put together in a labeled bag.

Talking Point 3: Naming of Template

The pattern name should be inscribed on each template piece just in case a piece happens to be misplaced. In addition, one should not forget to transfer any markings from the pattern pieces onto the templates. In conclusion, when using a plastic template, it's needful to mark the right side of the template to ensure that it is used correctly.

DESIGNING A QUILT

Talking Point 1: Sketching Made Easy by a Design.

A quilter is encouraged to sketch as way of practicing machine quilting. The knitter should practice sketching the quilting designs repeatedly until she becomes a master in it. Sketching the quilting designs teaches the knitter where to go next. Even though a quilter may not be an artist, one should train the brain to learn how a design looks like. A knitter can practice designs on a sewing machine by using paper on an unthreaded needle so as to have it established in mind.

Talking Point 2: What is in a Plan

It is essential to try and break down the quilt top into smaller components before picking out the quilting designs. For example, a particular quilt design consists of square blocks, a background, and a border. Quilt one design in the border in the background and a third one in the in the blocks. Quilt the same design in the background and border. Inside the blocks, you can decide to quilt different designs in the center and outside the blocks. This way, a quilter gets to know how many different quilting designs she requires for the quilt.

Talking Point 3: Quilting Different Types of Blocks

Blocks tend to make up the bulk of a quilt and can be the trickiest part of picking out quilting designs. Walking on quilts with the same block in a repeating pattern can make things easier. But sometimes, sampler quilts (quilts made up of various blocks) can drive the knitter for a loop in deciding on how to quilt different kinds of blocks. In choosing designs for the blocks, look no further than the block itself. Consider using the corners and edges as a guide for your quilting. This has a major advantage of minimal marking. One should avoid many markings on a quilt since removing the marks takes time as well. Continuous-curve quilting is a good example of using the block as a guide. Using the corners of a block as a reference point allows the quilter to quickly quilt curved lines from point to point, creating a straightforward design.

QUILTING IN NEGATIVE BLANK SPACE

Talking Point 1: What is Negative Blank Space in Quilting?

When a quilter says that her garment has negative blank space, a novice ends up confused.

Negative blank space is the region in a fabric that has not been quilted with any design in a quilted fabric. This negative blank space may appear in a block or the region around the block.

It falls within, about, or in between the quilted blocks. Thus, negative blank space comes off as an artistic pattern tool since it brings out the beauty of quilted pieces. At other times, the negative blank space in a piece of quilted piece merges with the pattern and thus becoming part of that garment in physical composition.

Though it carries a name showing negative effects, its use goes beyond determining the state, smooth flow, and appeal to the customers. Negative blank space also draws the appeal to the central focus while eye-catching to the enthusiast with its complex design.

Negative blank space can also produce an extra pattern

element in designs that are block-oriented patterns. In most block-oriented designs, the negative blank space forms a second pattern element or replicates the pattern in the positive spaces with the cartwheel quilt. The negative blank space replicates the cartwheel pattern.

The negative space between the blocks is a great place to experiment with extending the piecing. One can play around with it and come up with several different options. This technique not only allows the quilting to give the quilt a more cohesive look; it also gives you a whole range of ideas to try. Another plus is that since a quilter uses the quilt blocks as a guide, little to no marking is necessary. When dealing with large areas of negative space, the quilter is advised to use designs with movement to help create a dynamic and interesting look. Quilting designs that can add movement are relatively easy to see. They can have longer shapes or a fluid look. They can also include designs that vary in size.

Talking Point 2: Adding Texture to the Negative Space

In general, Pebble quilting is consistent in size, meaning that there isn't a lot of movement. As a result, pebbles are great for adding textures down the background. However, they probably shouldn't be the quilter's first choice if they want to add movement.

On the other hand, some elongated swirls reveal the stretched shape, fluid design, and varied sizes, which can add a lot of movement to large areas of negative space.

Another example of a quilting design with a lot of movement is called ogee, a name for a double-curved s shape. It has a lot of movement because the wavy horizontal lines move the quilter's eyes across the quilt, while the vertical lines create a beautiful texture. Another preferred way to quilt negative space is to extend the piercing with the quilting. A quilter should often look at a quilt top and imagine the piecing lines extending out and intersecting each other. Again, there are so many different options when a quilter approaches the quilt in this way.

Talking Point 3: Using Basic Quilting Designs in New And Unexpected Ways.

It would take forever to finish a quilt if a quilter tried to develop a new and original quilting design every time. Besides, that would take too much brainpower. So instead, a quilter should use free-motion quilting designs in new and surprising ways.

The first, and probably most important, the reason is that it's easy. Since a quilter already knows how to quilt the design, it doesn't take that much more effort to add a little tweak to create a different design. A good example is the boxy quilting design. Here a quilter could quilt this particular design in rows. This gives a uniform look to the background of a quilt. However, a quilter can use the design to give a different look by offsetting the squares and engaging a small, easy change that gives it a different look. Or a quilter could try tweaking her circles and seeing what she could come up with. If a quilter loves straight lines more than your taste, then she should try mixing up the directions. No matter how often a quilter tries switching up her favorite designs, the results are sure to be beautiful and enchanting.

COMPLEX QUILT BLOCKS

Talking Point 1: Quilting A Complex Quilt Block

Facing the task of quilting a complex quilt block can sometimes leave the quilter a little overwhelmed. However, realizing that the blocks break down into smaller shapes making picking out designs easier. Most blocks can be broken down into smaller shapes, like squares, triangles, and rectangles. When dealing with simpler shapes, it is easy to see that it's just a bunch of triangles and squares. This way, you can start picking out designs by focusing on ones that work well in triangles and squares.

Talking Point 2: Use of Contrast to Highlight Portions of Quilt Block.

When facing a block with many smaller pieces or a more complex pattern, consider highlighting just a portion of the block with a different quilting design. This improvised pieced quilt block is a good example. Instead of quilting each piece differently, quilt a basic swirl design and highlight the center of the block with a different design. When picking out contrasting quilting designs, find designs that are different in density and shape. For instance, quilting circular pebbles next to dense back and forth lines create contrast. Having contrast between the designs keeps them from blending. Want to change things up on your nest quilt? Try picking designs based on contrast, not on design.

Talking Point 3: Handling Borders in Quilt

Handling of borders can be a challenge when choosing quilting designs to use in the borders of the quilts; it is good to keep them as similar to the designs being in the middle of the quilt. This does not only feel cohesiveness to the quilt, but it is also easy to do. For a quilter to have the design already in mind means not thinking of a completely new design. For example, if you quilted back and forth lines in the main area of the quilt, try arranging them differently in the borders. In this example, it was as easy as quilting the back and forth lines on a diagonal, but with some spaces in between or vice versa. If you are quilting a large feather in the border of your quilt, you could use a feather meander in the main part of the quilt.
The End.

Did you like this book? Then you'll LOVE Knitting Essentials: How to Knit the Best Patterns for Beginners.

Knitting is an art that may confound many because it looks complex. But a closer look reveals that this art, where thread or yarn is used to create clothes, can be fascinating and soul-enriching if given its due attention. So I welcome you to the world of knitting, and I hope you will enjoy reading it as you try to unravel what looks like a mystery.

Knitting Essentials: How to Knit the Best Patterns for Beginners.

https://books2read.com/u/bzZ6v9

SNEAK PEEK - CHAPTER 1

Knitting Essentials: How to Knit the Best Patterns for Beginners.

https://books2read.com/u/bzZ6v9

Digital Cameras Are Here to Stay!

In a recent study conducted by Grand View Research a conclusion was reached that the global market for digital cameras is expected to grow to 19.77 billion units by 2020.

This will be driven by advancement in technology (including Wi-Fi cameras) as well as a surge in social networking. There are a number of other factors that will fuel this growth as well. Let's look at a few of them in closer detail.

. . .

•Digital cameras are "green technology" and friendly towards the environment. No chemicals are used for producing a photograph unlike in film photography.

•Digital cameras take more accurate pictures. Film cameras do not "see" the picture before it is shot in the same way a digital camera does. The electronics involved are able to adjust to take a better picture.

•No picture degradation. Negatives from conventional film can become scratched. As a digital photo is stored on a hard drive, the only risk is that the hard drive fails. Although backing up your data would prevent this.

•Taking a photo costs less. There is no need for film, developing or printing. Take a picture, store it on your computer and print it if you deem necessary.

Results are instant and can be used straight away.

•Press photographers at a sport's game take pictures of the ongoing action, and these are immediately sent to their newspapers to be published in hard copies and online.

•Instant photos mean you can learn as you take pictures, especially as a beginner photographer. The result of your shot is there to see immediately encourages you to try and use your camera and its various manual settings.

. . .

Digital cameras offer a massive advantage in storage.

•Images are first stored on the camera and, in all probability, will be moved to a computer hard drive. Compare this to normal photos which are found all over despite our best efforts to keep them in a central location.

•Only keep the photos you want. Photos that are not up to standard can be deleted.

•Photo editing. Some digital photos can be edited and manipulated. A normal photograph cannot.

•Digital photos are easy to share. In today's world of email and Facebook, sharing your pictures is easier than ever.

HOW A DIGITAL CAMERA WORKS

A digital camera is a fairly complex device. So let's take a look at how it all actually works.

A digital camera is similar to a conventional camera at the beginning of the photographic process. Lenses in the camera focus light to make an image of the scene being photographed.

. . .

Here the differences with a conventional camera start as the light is not focused onto film but on a semiconductor that records the light electronically and converts it into electrical charges.

Each digital camera has a certain resolution measured in pixels. This is the amount of detail a camera can capture in a photograph. The more pixels a camera has, the more detail it can capture in a photo without the photo losing quality and blurring or becoming grainy.

Resolutions on digital cameras can range from extremely low (1216 x 912, around 1 megapixel) to extremely high (4064 x 2704 or 11 megapixels). As digital camera technology constantly evolves, cameras with high megapixel resolutions are becoming available. When buying a camera, make sure it will take photos in a resolution that you will be happy with.

How Does a Digital Camera Capture Color?

When a digital camera records an image, it records the total intensity of the light in the scene. The camera sensors look at the light entering the unit in three primary colors using a filtering system to get full color. A full spectrum of color is created once the camera has recorded the three primary colors.

The capture process of the three primary colors can take place in a number of different ways, depending on the camera.

. . .

High quality digital cameras use three sensors, each having a different sensor where a beam splitter directs light.

Filters ensure that each sensor, although they "see" the whole image, only responds to the primary color assigned to them. Using this method, a digital camera records the three primary colors at each pixel location. Unfortunately, cameras using this method are expensive and rather large.

Another method can be used to capture color.

Red, green and blue filters are rotated in front of a single sensor. The sensor then records three separate images in succession. As the three images are not taken at the same moment, the camera and subject must remain still for all three readings.

Unfortunately, this is not very practical for handheld cameras.

These color capture methods are mostly used in digital cameras found in a professional photographic studio.

However, a far more cost-effective and practical method is used in smaller digital cameras.

Here a color filter array is placed over each light sensor that captures light as the photo is taken. The colors for the photo are recorded in a process called interpolation. With the sensors ordered into an assortment of red, blue, and green pixels, they get enough data from each other and accurately guess the true color of a certain part in the photograph.

These color array filters are normally found in a Bayer filter pattern. This is an alternating pattern of red and green filters and blue and green filters.

Interestingly, the pixels are not divided evenly. The green pixels outnumber the blue and red pixels by a ratio of 2:1. Why? Well, the human eye is not equally sensitive to all three colors, and more green pixels are needed to create an image our eyes see as true color.

This filter system's main advantage is that it only requires one sensor, and all color information is recorded simultaneously. Digital cameras with this system can therefore be smaller and cheaper to produce.

How Does a Digital Camera Handle Exposure & Focus?

In much the same way a conventional camera does, a digital camera controls the amount of light reaching the sensor using the aperture and shutter speed. However, unlike a conventional camera which has a mechanical shutter, a digital camera's shutter is operated digitally.

The aperture and shutter work in unison to ensure the correct amount of light is captured to make a great image. A digital camera's manual mode allows you to decide these settings for yourself.

Lenses in the camera also need to be adjusted to help control the light being focused on the sensor. Most digital camera lenses focus automatically.

Digital cameras normally have one of the following lens types:

•Fixed-focus, fixed-zoom lenses. These are limited but perfect for entry-level cameras which will be used for basic photography.

•Optical-zoom lenses with automatic focus. Here the photographer is able to choose between wide and telephoto options. Both of them will autofocus once the selection is made.

•Digital zoom lenses. Here the camera takes pixels from the image sensor and uses the interpolation method (explained above) to make a full-sized image.

•Replaceable lenses. Here the camera has a few options for lenses that can be used depending on the photographic situation.

How Does a Digital Camera Store Photos?

. . .

One advantage that a digital camera has over a conventional camera is its LCD screen that allows you to see your picture immediately after taking it. This allows you to delete the photos you do not like and keep the ones you do.

You are then able to move those pictures to a computer or directly to a printer for a hard copy.

Digital cameras today have a large number of options for photo storage. This can either be in the form of a fixed or removable flash memory, hard disks or microdrives, or writable mini CDs or DVDs.

Whatever the storage type, you will need a lot of space to store your photos. Cameras can store photos in a number of formats, including TIFF (uncompressed), JPEG (compressed), or RAW (a digital photo negative).

The table below shows you the size TIFF and JPEG formats in relation to the resolution of the camera taking it.

Camera Resolutions: 640 x 480 – 800 x 600 – 1024 x 768 – 1600 x 1200

Tiff Sizes: 1 MB – 1.5 MB – 2.5 MB – 6.0 MB

JPEG Sizes (Medium Quality) 90 KB - 130 KB – 200 KB - 420 KB

. . .

JPEG Sizes (High Quality) 300 KB - 500 KB - 800 KB – 1.7 MB

HOW DOES A DIGITAL CAMERA TAKE A PHOTO?

There are a number of steps in this process. Let's look at them a little closer. Please note this is for a digital camera in automatic mode.

- You find a subject to photograph, adjust the zoom.

- You press the shutter release button very lightly. This makes the camera automatically focus on your subject. The camera also gets a light reading at this point.

- The camera will set the aperture and shutter speed to get the best exposure for the photo.

- You press the shutter release down to take a photograph.

- The camera resets the sensor. It is then exposed to light while it builds up and electric charge until the shutter closes.

- The charge is measured, and a digital signal is created representing the value of the charge at each pixel.

- The camera processor creates natural color through the process of interpolation. At this stage you can view your photo on the cameras LCD screen.

. . .

- The photograph is stored in the cameras memory.

End of Sneak Peek

Knitting Essentials: How to Knit the Best Patterns for Beginners.

https://books2read.com/u/bzZ6v9

©Copyright 2022 – **All rights reserved by Jamie J.**

The content of this book may not be reproduced, duplicated, or transmitted without direct written permission from the author or publisher.

❦ Created with Vellum

www.ingramcontent.com/pod-product-compliance
Lightning Source LLC
LaVergne TN
LVHW021744060526
838200LV00052B/3452